THE JEWS AND RITUAL MURDERS OF CHRISTIAN BABIES

A Theological and Legal Study

by
Ippolit Iosifovich Lyutostansky
Ипполит Иосифович Лютостанский

The Jews and Ritual Murders of Christian Babies
by Ippolit Iosifovich Lyutostansky

ORIGINAL TITLE:
Жиды и ритуальныя убійства христіанскихъ младенцевъ
И.І. Лютостанскій

Third Russian edition, 1911.

Translation from Russian © 2016 by Alexander Onegin.
Published by permission.
Copyright © 2016 by Carlos Whitlock Porter. All rights reserved.

http://www.cwporter.com

Front cover: Saint Simon of Trent, a child ritually murdered by the Jews in 1475. Portrait attributed to Luca Ciamberlano. From a work published in 1607 by Pietro Stefanoni.

Table of Contents

Preface to the 2016 English Edition 5

Commendations 7

Author's Revelation 10

On the Murder of Andrei Yushchinsky in Kiev on the Eve
    of This Year's Easter 11

Abramova's Case of the Forcible Drawing of Her Child's Blood
    by the Jews in Smolensk on the Eve of Last Year's Easter 14

Historically and Legally Attested Ritual Murders 17

Saint Martyrs of the Christian Orthodox and
    Roman Catholic Churches 18

Court Verdict in Bela in the Case of the Murder of Parasza,
    a Christian Girl, by the Jews 20

Evidence as to the Existence of Jewish Ritual Murders 21

Newspaper Reports of Disappearances of Children 23

The Ritual Torturing and Murder of Saint Simon of Trent,
    a Catholic Child Martyr, by the Jews 26

The Murder of Fedor Emelyanov in Velizh 29

Verdict of the State Council in the Case of the Murder of Two
    Christian Boys by the Jews in Saratov 31

An Anxious Easter in Sofia 40

Fanatical Jewish Policy Against Christians 42

Saint Gavriil (Gabriel of Bialystok) 43

Other Monuments to Children Murdered by the Jews 45

Charters of Immunity Mentioning Ritual Murders 47

The Vilna Case of Vintsenta Grudzinskaya,
    Whose Blood Was Drawn by the Jews 50

On the Russian Names for the Jews 53

Favid (Favus), a Caste Disease of the Jews 54

A Jewish Murder in Kiev 56

THE JEWS

AND

RITUAL MURDERS

OF CHRISTIAN BABIES

A Theological and Legal Study

By Ippolit Iosifovich Lyutostansky

THIRD EDITION

EDITOR:
L.K. Popova

SANKT-PETERSBURG
Publishing House of the "SVET" Association
Nevsky Ave., No. 136

1911

Preface to the 2016 English Edition

Contrary to the universally held and politically correct opinion, Jewish ritual murders are not an "anti-Semitic prejudice" or an "evil blood libel" which originated in the dark Middle Ages, but are quite real and have existed for about 1,000 years. Nor is it true that confessions to such murders were always extorted under torture. The fact is that the reality of Jewish ritual murders, perpetrated by religious fanatics from the sect of the Hasidim, has been repeatedly proven in modern trials using modern rules of evidence, as it happened so many times in the Russian Empire in the 19th and early 20th century, before this country succumbed to Judeo-Bolshevik tyranny in 1917.

Quite a rich literature on this subject, dating back to the pre-Bolshevik period, exists in the Russian language. Two very important studies, *The Murder of Andrei Yushchinsky* by G.G. Zamyslovsky (1917) and *A Memorandum on Ritual Murders* by V.I. Dal (1844), were recently translated into English by JRBooksOnline and are available through Lulu.com.

The present short book was written by I.I. Lyutostansky in 1911 following the ritual murder of Andrei Yushchinsky, a 13-year old boy, in Kiev. Brief information on this and other ritual murder cases – which occurred both in Russia and abroad – is presented here.

Ippolit Iosifovich Lyutostansky (1835–1915) was an authoritative expert on the Jewish question, who gained fame due to his two major studies, *On the Use of Christian Blood by the Jews* and *The Talmud and the Jews*, which consisted of many volumes and went through numerous editions. He was highly praised for his works and received many commendations from high-ranking persons in Russia, including Emperor Alexander III and Empress Maria Feodorovna, a brave woman later murdered by the vindictive Jewish Bolsheviks, together with her husband, Emperor Nicholas II, and all their children.

Nicholas II was particularly hated by the Jews for his role in the famous Beilis trial. Mendel Beilis was a Jew accused of murdering Andrei Yushchinsky, a 13-year-old boy, in March 1911 in Kiev. His trial took place in the autumn of 1913 and attracted wide attention both in the Russian Empire and abroad. Eventually, Beilis was acquitted by the jury, but the same verdict also said that the murder was a ritual one and was committed at a Jewish brick factory. Now, it is quite obvious that this trial could not have happened without Nicholas II's will and involvement. Furthermore, the same Tsar, who wanted the evidence about Yushchinsky's murder to be preserved, reportedly commissioned G.G. Zamyslovsky to write the above-mentioned book. In 1918, Nicolas II would die a martyr's death, together with his entire family. Many decades later, they would be canonized by the Russian Orthodox Church, and since then they have been revered as martyrs.

After the Bolsheviks seized power in 1917, they destroyed all the copies of Lyutostansky's books they could lay their hands on, as well as those written by other authors, including Dal and Zamyslovsky. Also, they reportedly hunted down and shot not only those who had *read* Lyutostansky's books, but even those who had merely *heard* of them.

This brochure will become a valuable addition to the library of anyone interested in the Jewish question in general and Jewish ritual murders in particular. It is hoped by the editors that more books by this author will be published in English in the foreseeable future.

Carlos Whitlock Porter
December 2016

Commendations

From His Imperial Highness, Heir and Tsesarevich[1] Alexander Alexandrovich, Later His Imperial Majesty Alexander III The Peacemaker

Court of His Imperial Majesty,
Heir and Tsesarevich

From the Marshal of the Court
Court Office

April 14, 1876
No. 511
St. Petersburg

Copy

Dear Sir Ippolit Iosifovich,

    The HEIR AND TSESAREVICH has favorably received your work entitled *The Question of the Use of Christian Blood by the Jews (Sectarians) for Religious Purposes, in Connection with the Question of the Attitude of Jewry towards Christianity in General*, which had been attached to your letter to HIS IMPERIAL HIGHNESS from the 26th of this March, and has asked me to convey you the commendation of HIS HIGHNESS for the said gift.
    I have the honor to inform you about this wish of HIS IMPERIAL HIGHNESS.

Marshal of the Court, Zinovyev

Acting Head of the Court Office,
Aide-de-Camp of HIS HIGHNESS, Colonel Vasilkovsky

---

[1] Tsesarevich was the official title of the heir to the Russian throne. – *Translator's Note.*

Commendations

Marshal of the Court
of His Imperial Highness,
Heir and Tsesarevich

April 24, 1880
No. 777
St. Petersburg

Copy

Dear Sir Ippolit Iosifovich,

The HEIR AND TSESAREVICH has favorably received the second edition of your book entitled *On the Use of Christian Blood by the Jews*, and your work *The Talmud and the Jews*, which had been attached to your application from the 14th of this April, and has asked me, Dear Sir, to convey you the commendation of HIS IMPERIAL HIGHNESS for the said gift.

As I fulfill the wish of HIS HIGHNESS hereby, I would like to assure you of my absolute respect and esteem.

To His Most Honorable Sir
I.I. Lyutostansky   Your faithful servant, V. Zinovyev

Marshal of the Court
of His Imperial Highness,
Heir and Tsesarevich

August 29, 1880
No. 15000
St. Petersburg

Copy

Dear Sir Ippolit Iosifovich,

The HEIR AND TSESAREVICH has favorably received the third volume of your work *The Talmud and the Jews*, which had been attached to your application to HIS IMPERIAL HIGHNESS from the 22nd of this August, and has asked me, Dear Sir, to convey you the commendation of His Highness for the said gift.

Commendations

As I fulfill the wish of HIS IMPERIAL HIGHNESS hereby, I would like to assure you of my absolute respect and esteem.

To His Most Honorable Sir
I.I. Lyutostansky   Your faithful servant, V. Zinovyev

The author was privileged to receive from Emperor Alexander III, as a gift, an album with a Tsar's portrait, adorned with velvet and gold, with the Tsar's initials, where commendations from Tsars, Tsarinas and many Great Princes, along with two dozens of commendations from ministers, generals and scholars, for presenting them the unique books in Russia, are kept.

Author's Revelation

Although I published a study of the Talmud, and a theological and legal study of the ritual murders of Christian babies by the Jews, I am not their enemy, but rather I pity them. For this reason, I ask my Christian Orthodox brothers not to nourish feelings of hatred and malice towards the Jews, and particularly to refrain from violent and arbitrary reprisals. I recommend them to act according to the words of [Ion C.] Bratianu, a clever Romanian minister, who reproached the Romanian people for carrying out a Jewish pogrom. Bratianu said: "Do not commit any violence or pogroms against the Jews, for it would only harm *you*. Instead, create solidarity among yourselves so as not to buy anything from the Jews, or sell anything to them, or take service with them. Then, even if you wanted to make them stay, they would run away from you."

A new edition of our books is an absolute necessity for crime investigation commissions. This is shown by the Vilna case involving a Jew named Blondes, who was accused of forcibly drawing blood from a Christian girl in 1900, and who was eventually convicted. The Public Prosecutor of the Judicial Court, as he investigated the case, searched for our book *On the Use of Christian Blood by Jewish Sectarians* in the whole of Vilna, offered 100 rubles for it, but was unable to find the only legal study available in Russia that sheds light on ritual murders perpetrated by Jewish fanatics since the early centuries of the Christian epoch and up to the most recent times.

We can name fourteen cases which took place [between 1890 and 1900], where the Jews were accused of using Christian blood, beginning with the famous story that occurred on the island of Corfu in 1891[1], and ending with the Konitz trial[2] and the Polna trials[3].

Ritual murders have recently produced a whole literature in Germany. Those who wish to familiarize themselves with this issue are referred to the first volume of our book *On the Use of Christian Blood by Jewish Sectarians*, which contains a German bibliography on ritual murders for 1890 to 1900.

---

[1] Greece, murder of an 8-year-old girl. – *Translator's Note*.
[2] West Prussia, murder of a young man in 1900. – *Translator's Note*.
[3] Bohemia, murder of two young girls in 1898 and 1899. – *Translator's Note*.

On the Murder of Andrei Yushchinsky in Kiev on the Eve of This Year's Easter

The murder of Andrei Yushchinsky aroused great indignation and excitement in Kiev after the details of the torture-murder became known. The Jews became particularly agitated and started spreading a rumor that the boy was killed by his own mother. When it turned out that there was no evidence against the mother whatsoever, and especially when it was clearly established that several persons had participated in the murder, the Jews changed their tactic, and a new rumor is now being intensely spread throughout the city, namely that Yushchinsky's murder was allegedly committed by the "unionists"[1] and was "a provocation made by the extreme right forces in order to incite pogroms". The Jews back up this thesis in a very original way. They say: "Since the establishment of the new judicial institutions, this is the only murder in which all the ritual requirements described in books dealing with Jewish ritual murder were meticulously complied with – down to the minutest detail, with great accuracy. It is therefore clear that before committing the crime, the murderers studied the rite from books; and this could only have been done by the unionists." Although the Jews are persistently spreading this rumor, they are having no success, for their tale is too absurd.

At the same time, the Jews are trying hard to persuade both the local authorities and the influential representatives of Russian society that there is no such thing as Jewish ritual murders. The only argument brought forward is this: "For goodness' sake, how could such murders possibly take place in the 20th century?!" Particularly active has been David Margolin, the head of the Kiev Jews and a millionaire (he is a favorite of the local top-level administration which has repeatedly nominated him for the rank of active state councilor). Margolin even went cap in hand to the Volhynia province to meet a Russian personality who is very influential in Kiev, and asked him to protect "the poor Kiev Jews". Following that, a meeting of influential representatives of the local Russian society took place in the apartment of a high-ranking official of the Ministry of Finances. David Margolin and a rabbi came to this meeting and started arguing that there is no

---

[1] Members of the Union of the Russian Nation and other patriotic organizations. – *Translator's Note*.

such thing as Jewish ritual murders. They mentioned the Torah (the Five Books of Moses), which says not a word about ritual murders. To this, it was pointed out that, firstly, no one accuses the Jews as a whole of committing ritual murders: such murders, as it has been established with certainty, are only perpetrated by the sect of the Hasidim, which includes the most ignorant and sadistic part of Jewry; and secondly, the Torah is part of the Old Testament, while Hasidic ritual murders appeared after the coming of the Savior.

Seeing that they could not fool the representatives of the Russian population, the Jews transferred their activity to administrative circles. They started beating down the doors of all kinds of public officials. As a matter of fact, the latter had taken great fright anyway. During the first two or three weeks, the authorities did not even bother to investigate the crime and find the murderers; all they did was protect the "poor" Jews against any kind of offence. "To avoid a pogrom at any cost" – this was the only concern of the authorities. A clear intention to hush up the whole matter became manifest. Things went so far that police officers went throughout the city and tried to persuade people that the murder had proven to be *not* a ritual one. The results were quite the opposite: the Russian population was not calmed down, but rather became irritated and indignant. Everyone talked about the terrible power of Jewry, that the authorities obeyed the Jews, etc.

Who knows how the matter would have ended, had it not been for the chivalrously straightforward and tactful measures undertaken by the governor [of the Kiev province], A.F. Girs. He demanded that the local administration (the detective police, the provincial gendarmerie, etc.) use all means and efforts to find the murderers. After that, the governor issued an appeal to the influential representatives of local patriotic organizations, informing them about all the measures which had been undertaken (unfortunately, quite late) to discover the murderers. This had a very beneficial effect. The Russian population, as it learned about the radical shift in the attitude of the authorities towards the horrible crime, immediately calmed down. It is a shame that A.F. Girs had not been in Kiev during the first weeks after the murder had become known.

Naturally, the Jews did not grow quiet but, on the contrary, intensified their efforts. It would have seemed that since Jewry as a whole is not guilty of ritual crimes, the Jews should have sought to find the murderers and establish all the details of the crime, and had it turned out that the culprits were sadistic sectarians, the Jews should have handed them to the authorities and repudiated them. This is how the Russian nation treats its own sadistic sectarians, and it is the best way to fight against them. However, instead of doing this, the Jews try to obscure the case and vigorously defend the Hasidic sectarians.

Jewish efforts in this regard became particularly manifest when the representatives of the Russian population wanted to hold a memorial service at the grave of the murdered boy. The Public Prosecutor of the Judicial Court insisted that the service be prohibited. The Jews insistently demanded the same. A.F. Girs strongly objected to such a prohibition, believing that this measure would anger and insult the Russian population. The memorial service did take place, and despite the lack of any preliminary announcements, several thousand people attended it. There were no incidents during the service. Those present decided to collect funds for the erection of a proper monument on the boy's grave. For the time being, a temporary metallic monument was installed there.

The search for the murderers has been fruitless so far. This is hardly a surprise, because the investigation authorities had done almost nothing at first, until the case was entrusted to V.I. Fenenko, an energetic and talented special investigator, while the Jews have been feverishly working from the very beginning. Most probably, all the traces of the culprits were covered up already.

The investigation of the crime and the ascertainment of its nature have been greatly hindered by a real terror unleashed by the Jews. Many persons involved in the judicial and investigation proceedings are overwhelmed with fear – fear of revenge and reprisal on the part of Jewry. It is being said that the Jews have collected huge amounts of money in order to hush up the case. The record of past ritual murders shows that the Jews have always known how to get rid of those preventing them to hush up such cases. V.I. Fenenko is a fearless man, but non-Jewish residents of Kiev are afraid he could be suddenly transferred to another place (maybe even with a promotion), as it used to happen before. The Jews are extremely powerful.[1]

---

[1] See more about the Yushchinsky case in the brilliant book *The Murder of Andrei Yushchinsky* by G.G. Zamyslovsky, recently published in English by JRBooksOnline.com, 2016. – *Translator's Note.*

Abramova's Case of the Forcible Drawing of Her Child's Blood by the Jews in Smolensk on the Eve of Last Year's Easter

A Christian woman by the name of Abramova came begging to the Jewish family of Pinkus, with her child [a girl] in her arms. There, the child was taken from her on a plausible pretext, carried away to another half of the house, and only brought back after a very long time, when Abramova started crying and asking the Jews to give her child back.

When Pinkus, a Jewish woman, trembling all over, brought the child, gave it to Abramova and hurriedly led her out of the house, it turned out that the child had been *pricked all over with some tool* and was deathly pale – it was dying.

Abramova's story is a typical example of such cases. The additional information we have obtained leaves no doubt as to the true goal of the Jews, who bestially tortured the child.

To start with, on March 5, as she was begging, Abramova came to Chernyak, a petty Jewish salesman who lived in the district under the jurisdiction of the 3rd Police Precinct of the town of Smolensk.

Chernyak, who had usually refused Abramova in a coarse manner, this time tenderly received her, *gave her tea*, and recommended her to go to the Jewish family of Pinkus and Blyumenshteyn (Pinkus' brother-in-law [or son-in-law[1]]), who lived nearby on the same street, and who allegedly would also "receive her well".

So Abramova went to the Pinkuses, and the result was a mercilessly disfigured and dying child. Witnesses in this matter maintain that the plan to decoy Abramova and use her child for mean purposes had been thought out by the Jews in advance. This is evidenced by Chernyak's cordial welcome of Abramova. Later, Abramova would come to Chernyak, weeping and asking him why he sent her to the Pinkuses.

The Smolensk doctors refused to help Abramova and told her not to "kick up a fuss", while in the 3rd Police Precinct of Smolensk she was literally chucked out – many people saw Abramova crying after receiving such "support".

It was only in late April that Abramova was fortunate to meet a good and decent man, P. Gavrilov, who vigorously started working on

---

[1] The same word in Russian. – *Translator's Note.*

her case. First of all, Gavrilov asked Abramova to show him the Jews who had tortured her child.

Abramova brought him to the Pinkuses' house, where they found a whole company of the Jews celebrating a wedding.

Pinkus, the Jewish woman who, shivering as if from fever, had brought the child to Abramova on March 5 after the bloodletting, as she saw Abramova, *fainted with a cry*.

After visiting the Pinkuses, Gavrilov went to the 3rd Police Precinct and filed a complaint on Abramova's behalf. Interestingly, *the police officer insistently tried to persuade Gavrilov not to file the complaint*.

Following that, the Jews from the Pinkus family came to the police, and *after talking with the superintendent of the 3rd Police Precinct*, they approached Gavrilov and started asking him not to involve himself in Abramova's case, assuring him that *Abramova was crazy* and the police would soon send her to a lunatic asylum.

Abramova started sobbing and said: "Send me anywhere you want, but you did prick my child all over!"

At Gavrilov's insistence, the superintendent registered the complaint and sent Abramova with her child to a doctor named Khodorovsky for a medical examination. Now, Khodorovsky would write in his report that "marks are present on the child's body in various places" (their exact number was given), but, according to the same report, *he could not establish their origin*.

Nice, is it not? He could *not* establish that detail, but he *could* lie when he wrote at the end of his report that according to her mother's words, the girl "suffered from boils", *although Abramova had told him nothing of this sort*. Furthermore, according to the testimonies of numerous persons who closely knew Abramova, *the child had been very healthy and ruddy-complexioned* before being subjected to the Jewish bloodletting.

Finally, the case reached Kryukov, the Public Prosecutor of the Smolensk District Court, who would charge Tkachev, the head of the detective department, to interrogate Abramova. I must conclude that this step on Kryukov's part was a serious mistake, for everyone knows what kind of role is played by heads of detective departments in towns with a numerous Jewish population, starting with Mikheyev in Samara, and ending with Matveyev in Kherson or the Kiev kingpins of the detective business whose names recently resounded throughout Russia[1].

Tkachev, reckoning that Abramova's daughter, exhausted by the colossal loss of blood, would die soon, resorted to bureaucratic trickery.

---

[1] Allusion to the Yushchinsky case. – *Translator's Note*.

Abramova lives in Smolensk, and every little Jew knows her place of residence (small wonder), which is also recorded in the 3rd Police Precinct's register. However, according to her passport, Abramova is a peasant of the Vladimir volost[1] of the Smolensk province. So Tkachev, this worthy new-fashioned jack-in-office, sent a subpoena to Abramova, by registered letter, *to the Vladimir Volost Administration*! A nice trick, is it not? This police fruit from the bureaucratic gardens of the new administration, this "noble", "honest" and "incorruptible" servant of the oppressed *Inorodtsy*[2], simply had no way of knowing where Abramova lived, despite him being *the head of the detective department*! You may rest assured that Tkachev received nothing from the Pinkuses for delaying Abramova's interrogation.

As a result, the subpoena sent by Tkachev has still not been received by the Vladimir Volost Administration.

But what is most interesting is that shortly after Tkachev had sent his subpoena to Abramova, the superintendent of the 3rd Police Precinct suddenly received a happy news: Abramova's child died. The superintendent – delighted with this surprise which had so quickly, easily and ultimately brought the murder case to an end – summoned Abramova... no, not by sending a subpoena to the Vladimir Volost Administration by registered letter in Tkachev's imitation; he simply *sent a policeman to Abramova's apartment*.

In this revolting manner was Abramova's case dismissed. In conclusion, we would like to congratulate the Smolensk governor from the bottom of our hearts for such a brilliant selection of town police agents – they are very nice fellows!

---

[1] A peasant community in Tsarist Russia consisting of several villages or hamlets. – *Translator's Note*.

[2] A term applied in the Russian Empire to certain non-Slavs, including the Jews. – *Translator's Note*.

Historically and Legally Attested Ritual Murders

1) In 168 B.C., Antiochus Epiphanes, a Syrian king, as he was devastating the Jerusalem Temple, came across a secret room, where a Greek lay on a bed. The Greek asked the king to save him: he had been decoyed into the Temple and held there against his will. After insistent questions, the servants told the king that the Jews had a secret law which commanded them to offer human sacrifice each year at a certain time (Josephus, *Contra Apionem*).

2) In the 4th century A.D., during the rule of Roman Emperor Constantine the Great, the Jews were expelled from several provinces for crucifying a Christian child on a cross on Good Friday. Furthermore, during the rule of Theodosius II, the Jews were forbidden to celebrate their feasts by mocking a resemblance of a cross, which they had used to burn solemnly. The Jews were also forbidden to build synagogues in secluded places, so as to prevent various atrocities which had repeatedly occurred. Nevertheless, the Jews would still secretly *crucify* Christian babies, and several of their people were executed for that, as it happened in 419 in Syria, between Antioch and Chalcedon, at Inmestar (Eisenmenger, *Entdecktes Judenthum*, vol. 2).

3) During the reign of Phocas, the Jews were expelled from Antioch for murdering Bishop Anastasius I of Antioch and many other Christians for sadistic reasons (a history of the Church in Polish).

An extensive list of similar cases can be found in our book *On the Use of Christian Blood by the Jews for Religious Purposes* (3rd ed., vol. 1, pp. 89–129, cases 4–145, up to year 1900).[1] Those who want to familiarize themselves with these historical and legal cases (including the corresponding verdicts and executions) can consult the said work, published in two volumes and approved by Russian scholarly, civil and military committees.

---

[1] Most of these cases were taken from *A Memorandum on Ritual Murders* by V.I. Dal. This short book, too, was recently published in English by JRBooksOnline.com, 2016. – *Translator's Note*.

Saint Martyrs of the Christian Orthodox and Roman Catholic Churches

According to the data provided by various authoritative historians, 86 Christian children were murdered by the Jews outside Poland from 415 to 1699, and 68 children were murdered in Poland from 1407 to 1710. The total number of the martyrs is 154.

The following martyrs, killed by the Jews, were canonized by the <u>Christian Orthodox Church</u>:

1) Saint Eustratius, whose relics are kept in the Kiev Pechersk Lavra. This monk from Kiev was crucified by the Jews on a cross on Good Friday, during the rite of the mockery of Jesus Christ, in 1096. A detailed description can be found in *On the Use of Christian Blood...*, vol. 1.

2) Saint Gavriil[1], a baby murdered in 1690, whose relics repose in the Holy Trinity Orthodox Monastery in Slutsk[2]. A detailed description, with church hymns and a hagiography, is found in the above-mentioned work, vol. 1.

The following martyrs, also killed by the Jews, were canonized by the <u>Roman Catholic Church</u>:

1) Saint William, murdered in 1144 in Norwich, England.

2) Saint Rudolf, murdered in 1183 in Paris, France.

3) Saint Hugh, murdered in 1255 in Lincoln, England.

4) Saint Werner, murdered in 1287 in Bacharach, present-day Germany.

5) Saint Konrad, murdered in 1303 in Weißensee, Thuringia.

6) Saint Simon, murdered in 1475 in Trent, Tirol.

7) Saint Wojtaszek, murdered in 1550 in Kodna [?], a Czech town.

In 1598, with the blessing of the Holy See, monuments in memory of a large number of child martyrs were erected, and their coffins were placed in many churches. They are remembered by the Catholic Church in its prayers on the anniversary of their martyrdom.[3]

---

[1] Generally known as Gabriel of Bialystok or Gavriil Belostoksky. His memory is still celebrated by the Orthodox Church. – *Translator's Note*.

[2] This monastery was demolished by the Communists after 1917. Saint Gavriil's relics are currently kept in Saint Nicholas' Cathedral in Bialystok, Poland. – *Translator's Note*.

[3] This is no longer the case. Most (if not all) of the mentioned Catholic martyrs were removed from the list of saints. – *Translator's Note*.

In *Lives of the Saints* by Piotr Skarga[1], a Roman Catholic priest, we also find a biography of Elzbieta, a girl tortured to death by the Jews in 1574 in the town of Punia, Lithuania, 12 miles from Vilna, over the Neman River.

In 1171, the abbot of Mont-Saint-Michel bitterly complained of the Jews, and he was echoed by Count Thibaut de Chartres, who burned several Jews at the stake for crucifying a baby during Easter. At about the same time, the Jews made another victim in Pontoise, under the walls of Paris[2]. This martyr of the Roman Catholic Church is no less famous as William of Norwich from England. This country, too, cried out because of the Jews, despite it being separated from France by the sea. The same violent crimes occurred there as well, and the Church confirms these facts, witnessed by the two rival countries and corroborated by documentary evidence.

---

[1] *Zywoty swietych*, 1st Polish edition, 1579. – *Translator's Note.*
[2] This must refer to Richard of Pontoise, a boy crucified by the Jews. – *Translator's Note.*

Court Verdict in Bela in the Case of the Murder of Parasza, a Christian Girl, by the Jews

On April 12, 1710, Paliutik[1], a philanderer, sold a girl named Parasza to the Jews for twenty groszy. Her unburied corpse would be found behind the house of her Jewish murderer, Zelik (the Jews always throw away the corpses of their victims as carrion, for they are forbidden to bury them). As the corpse was examined, it turned out that the body had been pricked all over with some thin and sharp tool. On the cheeks, near the ears, and below the knees, the veins had been cut open and bandages had been applied to squeeze out the blood. The culprit was given away by the girl's dress discovered in the shed, that is, on the place where the girl had been tortured. The Jewish murderer virulently denied everything, even if Paliutik himself, the one who had sold the child, directly exposed him. Under torture, the Jew persisted as well and did not confess to anything. Nevertheless, in view of strong evidence, the court sentenced both criminals, Paliutik and Zelik, to death. (Stefan Zuchowski, *Proces kryminalny o niewinne dziecie Jerzego Krasnowskiego...*, 1713.)

In a similar case in Lublin, the Jews were sentenced to execution to be carried out on Saturday, and a scaffold was erected opposite the very synagogue. However, following strong Jewish solicitations, this part of the court verdict was overturned, and the execution was performed in a different place. From Sleszkowski's book, we learn that after all Jewish efforts to overturn the verdict had proved fruitless, the Jews went to Jesuit fathers and implored them as follows: "Holy Fathers, we are asking for clemency, please have mercy on us." And as the Jesuits were building their church in Lublin at that time, the Jews offered them 400 zlotys – of course, not for vacating the death sentence (asking for that would obviously have been useless), but only for not carrying out the execution in front of the synagogue. (Sebastian Sleszkowski, *Odkrycie zdrad...*, Brunsberga [Braniewo], 1621.)

---

[1] This and some other names appearing in this chapter could be written differently in Polish. They were written phonetically in Russian, using the Cyrillic alphabet. – *Translator's Note*.

Evidence as to the Existence of Jewish Ritual Murders

Prince Radziwill attests that "a converted rabbi from Nesvizh argued, by quoting from the Talmud, that the Jews use Christian blood".

Jan Serafinowicz, a former Lithuanian senior rabbi, who was later baptized, testified under oath in the Sandomierz Consistory Court that "the Jews cannot do without Christian blood".

Some scholars maintain that Jewish ritual murders are caused by the following prophecy of Rabbi Rav Ashi: "The flame of fierce enmity and revenge on the part of Christians could only be quenched with their own blood, by secret sacrificial offerings of innocent babies."

"Ritual murders are implied by the Talmudic book of *Chochmes-Nister*[1], although not quite clearly," says Gaudenty Pikulski.

"By murdering the children of the *Akum* (Christians), the Jews murder Christ in them." (*Sanhendrin*, VI, 48; VII, 2 and 508; *Abodah Zarah*, II, 9, etc.)

In a book entitled *Talmudic Tales*, published in 1794 in the Pochaev Monastery, it says that "during the month of Nissan [April], the Jews torture Christian babies if they can get them, and that this is mentioned by the Talmudic books of *Zevchelev* and *Chochmes*[2]; and the Jews need the blood of Christian babies for sacrificial reconciliation with God".

In the Talmudic treatise *Iore Dea* (section 66, sheet 53), it says: "The blood of cattle, animals and birds is forbidden; the blood of fish and human blood, which are not forbidden by the law, are allowed in any mixture with food."

The book of *Shulchan Aruch* (p. 42, verse 67) also clearly says the same: "The blood of cattle and animals cannot be consumed as food, but human blood can [be consumed as food], for our good. The *Goim* were warned long ago, but we cannot do without their blood for [the purposes] mentioned in the treatise *Tosafot*." The same treatise (p. 119, verse 193) says: "Do not befriend a Christian where you need to... so that they would not learn about the shedding of blood."

---

[1] Mistake in the name of the treatise. – *I.I. Lyutostansky*. (Possibly, *Choshen ha-Mishpat*. – *Translator's Note*.)

[2] A mistake. – *I.I. Lyutostansky*. (*Chochmes* could stand for *Choshen [ha-Mishpat]*. – *Translator's Note*.)

In the archives of the Ministry of Internal Affairs, there is an extract from a Jewish book entitled *Etz Hayim* (*Tree of Life*), written in the 17th century by Rabbi Chaim Vital. Here is the translation of this extract:

"Any animal preserves a certain particle of the Almighty's holiness by way of life, and a man, whoever he is, preserves this holiness during his life more than an animal does. When we slaughter an animal, the shadow of life leaves it, together with a certain particle of holiness, and [goes to] the one who consumes this animal as food; but before the shadow of life has completely detached from the animal, the certain particle of holiness left in it forbids us to consume it as food. The same is said in the Holy Scripture about a man as well (Numbers 14:9): 'We will devour them, for their shadow [protection] is gone.' This hints to us that since that particle of holiness is no longer in them, they are like slaughtered animals or bread which we should eat (devour); therefore, it is said (Numbers 23:24): 'The people [Israel]... does not rest till it devours its prey and drinks the blood of its victims,' and this is a hint at people who do not preserve holiness from above in them. From all of this, we conclude that through murdering a *Goi* [a Christian] and drinking his blood, the holiness of Israel and the Jews grows."

Directly related to ritual murders are also such secret Jewish books as *The Chronicle of the Blessed Moses, the Founder of Our Faith*, the Zohar, *Sefer ha-Likutim*, the Passover *Haggadah*, and others.

Newspaper Reports
of Disappearances of Children

In the [St. Petersburg] *Novoye Vremya* newspaper (No. 11145), we read:
"On March 22, the Gavansky police precinct was informed about the disappearance of two children, an 11-year-old boy Volodya and a 6-year-old girl Zhenya, living on Maly Ave., 26-13. The children had been clad in blue overcoats, along with caps and buttoned boots. They had gone out of their house on the previous day."

Peterburgskaya Gazeta (1893, No. 79) reported an unsuccessful attempt to kidnap a Christian child:
"On March 20, Mrs. V., a staff captain's wife, was walking on Bolshoi Vasileostrovsky Ave. with a 7-year-old son and a 3-year-old daughter. She stopped at a street corner to buy some trinket from a vendor. Her son saw a dog sitting by the vendor, and started petting it.

"When after 2 or 3 minutes Mrs. V. turned around to take the children in her arms, she could not see her daughter. The scared mother started looking in all directions, calling her daughter by name: 'Lida, Lida!'

"A cabman standing nearby said that he had seen how a woman of Jewish appearance had taken the child in her arms and had hurried away to the left, towards the Neva embankment. He had thought she was an acquaintance of Mrs. V.'s, for she had been following Mrs. V. and had stopped at the same corner.

"Alarmed at her daughter's disappearance, Mrs. V. asked the cabman to pursue the unknown woman, and on the Neva embankment, near the Mining Institute, she noticed a woman in a red skirt, who was quickly walking with a child struggling in her arms.

"Mrs. V. started shouting. The woman turned around and, noticing the pursuit, put the girl down and ran away, alone, towards the Maslyany islet, where she eventually disappeared, before the mother, rejoicing at finding her daughter, could further pursue her."

In the *Svet* newspaper (No. 80), the following news item appeared:

"Two boys, of 3 and 6 years of age, disappeared without a trace in Kharkov; one boy disappeared in Taganrog; two children, in St. Petersburg; and two boys, in Taraz [Talas]. All these disappearances oddly coincided with the first days of the Jewish feast of Passover, and gave rise to new rumors of ritual murders throughout Russia."

In the [Russian] *Kolokol* newspaper, the following report entitled "Sadistic Murder of a Baby by the Jews in Port Said[1]" was published:

"Recently, the citizens of Port Said strongly revolted against the Jews. The ground for the revolt had been prepared, to a considerable degree, by the behavior of the Palestinian Jewish emigrants, on the one hand, and, on the other hand, by the unrest in Alexandria, when, following the unsuccessful expropriation of a Russian steamship, the mob had torn away the signboard of the Russian consulate.

"Local residents believe [the child was kidnapped] by the Jewish emigrants who had poured in from Russia.

"The news of the boy's disappearance, rapidly spreading from mouth to mouth, agitated all the citizens. The long concealed feeling of animosity was about to burst out at any moment. Everyone noticed that the boy's disappearance coincided with the beginning of a Jewish feast. Similar cases of ritual murders which had occurred on the island of Corfu or elsewhere were recalled.

"Eventually, the boy's mutilated body was found on the shore of the As Salchanat Lake."

In 1907, in *Novoye Vremya*, two letters to the editorial office were published. Those were screams of despair of unfortunate parents whose children, two boys, had disappeared. One boy had lived in Baku, and the other, in St. Petersburg.

Peterburgskaya Gazeta (1894, No. 103) reports similar incidents:

"Several wires have been sent to police precincts, demanding them to take measures for finding several young girls of 10 to 16 years of

---

[1] A city in Egypt. – *Translator's Note.*

age, who had disappeared at various times during this week. Particular efforts should be made by the police to find Marie Le Hoff, the daughter of a French citizen; she had disappeared three days ago as she had been going to church. It is believed that the girls had been kidnapped by the Jews."

Somewhat later, newspapers reported that several corpses of the disappeared children, with all the signs of ritual murder, were found on Semenovsky Plats[1].

---

[1] A square in St. Petersburg. – *Translator's Note*.

The Ritual Torturing and Murder of Saint Simon of Trent, a Catholic Child Martyr, by the Jews

(Taken from *Lives of the Saints* by Piotr Skarga)

In 1475, in the city of Trent[1], three Jewish house owners, Jacob[2], Anel and Samuel, lived. Shortly before Passover, on Tuesday of Holy Week, these three Jews gathered in Samuel's house, and as they talked, Anel said:

"We have almost everything for this feast, both fish and meat, but one thing is still missing."

"What is that?" asked Samuel.

As they glanced at each other, they understood everything: Christian blood was missing; they needed a Christian child for a sacrificial offering. The Jews use a Christian child, if they can get or kidnap one, for mocking Christ; they kill it in a barbaric manner and use its blood for various sacrilegious rites. They call this blood *Ioel*, that is, "jubilee".

They did not say anything to their servants. On the next day, as these Jews gathered together again, they would discuss the same thing, but openly this time. As Samuel's house was large, it was decided to make the offering in his house; all they needed was to get a Christian baby, and it was the main subject they discussed on that day. Samuel called his servant Lazarus and tried to persuade him to get them a Christian baby, offering him 100 coins for that right away. However, the servant categorically refused this offer, saying that it would be a difficult and dangerous affair. As he left the room, Lazarus hurriedly packed his things and departed from the city.

On Thursday, the Jews gathered in the synagogue and told a Jew named Tobias:

"No one other than you could do it: you know many Christians, and you often walk around the city, so you could easily decoy some child to us, and we all would be very grateful to you for that."

---

[1] A city in South Tyrol, modern-day Italy. – *Translator's Note*.

[2] Again, some names from this chapter could have been written differently in the original. – *Translator's Note*.

Tobias tried to refuse this hard duty which was being imposed upon him, but they reminded him of a vow [he had once taken]. At last, being enticed with promises of great rewards, and most importantly, due to his hatred towards Christians, he promised them to honor their request. He then told Samuel:

"Do not shut your doors during this day and night, so that I could more easily bring you a Christian child at any moment."

By the same evening, Tobias, as he was looking for a proper child and waiting for a convenient time to carry out his intention, walked by Fossato [?] Street. There, he noticed a very handsome child named Simon, of 2.5 years of age, a son of poor parents Adriano and Maria, who was sitting near his parents' house. The Jew gave him his hand, and the tender child credulously accepted it. Tobias pulled the child along, saying he would bring him to his mother. However, after they passed the boy's house, he started crying, so the Jew gave him some money and sweets in order to calm him down. In this manner, he brought the child to Samuel's house and shoved him inside. Samuel, who had been waiting for this with great impatience, picked up the child and immediately hid him until night.

The mother quickly noticed her child was missing and started searching for him, but, of course, she would not find him. Suspicion fell on the Jews, and everyone said it was they who had kidnapped the boy. People wanted to make a search in the Jewish houses, but just as they were about to do so, night fell.

Great was the joy of the Jews when they entered the narthex of their synagogue on that night, for they had succeeded in procuring a victim. Taking the innocent baby, Samuel removed his clothes, tied his mouth with a kerchief so that he would not scream, and tied his neck up as well. Telling the others to hold the child by his arms and legs, and stretching him over a wide basin, he took a knife and slightly cut a vein near the throat. The blood was flowing into the basin. Picking up a pair of scissors, Samuel started cutting small pieces of flesh from the boy's face, putting them into the basin; then, the same was done by all the other Jews by turns. Next, Samuel took the child's right leg and, again, cut small pieces of living flesh, this time under the knee; the others would do the same. After that, Tobias sat down near Samuel, asked the half-dead boy to be given to him, and stretching him crosswise together with Samuel, told everyone to prick the boy with two needles, from the head to the legs. God alone witnessed how the Jews tortured the little child, while singing:

"Just as we killed Jesus, the Christian God, so will we kill this boy, and may all our enemies be disgraced forever!"

The Jews kept pricking the child with needles until the last signs of life were gone. This continued for about an hour. After they murdered the victim, the Jews happily thanked God for having been able to take revenge on God's and their own enemies. Samuel ordered the martyr's body to be hidden in a wine barrel, and everyone left to have supper.

On the next day, on Good Friday, people searched for the boy together with the police, made announcements in the streets and marketplaces, and even searched in the river, in case he had drowned, but everything was in vain.

On Saturday, as the Jews assembled in the synagogue, the corpse of the murdered child was crucified on the bimah, a place from which the Torah is read, and after holding a thanksgiving service, they hid the martyr's body in the same place for the time being.

On Sunday, seeing that everyone suspected them, the Jews held a council as to where they should hide the body, and decided to put clothes on it and throw it into the small river which flowed near their houses, and where the river was barred by an iron grating. They thought that if the body would be stopped by the iron grating, they could justify themselves by claiming that the corpse had been brought to their houses by water; and should nobody notice it, that would be the end of the whole matter. However, they had been so blinded by the innocent blood that they actually gave themselves away.

At that time, Johannes Hinderbach was the bishop of the city. When one of the murderers, Tobias, came to him to say that the child's body had been brought by water to their synagogue and had gotten stuck in the grating, the bishop told Jacob of Sporo [?], the mayor of Trent, and Jean de Salis, the city judge, to go to the river and verify everything the Jew had told them. They went there, and indeed found the corpse of the child martyr, which they took to Saint Peter's church. Then, they arrested the Jewish culprits and subjected them to interrogations. They all confessed to the murder and gave a detailed account of everything, testifying against each other and trying to shift the blame for the crime on the others, but eventually they got confused and explained the matter in greater detail. The local judicial authorities sentenced the culprits to death in accordance with the strict laws. Simon was canonized by the Roman Catholic Church, and his relics still repose in Saint Peter's church in Trent.[1]

---

[1] Just like the other children ritually murdered by the Jews, Simon of Trent was recently removed from the Roman Martyrology. – *Translator's Note*.

The Murder of Fedor Emelyanov in Velizh

As we are unable to discuss all the trials of this kind herein, we will confine ourselves to two of them.

The first trial took place in the Russian town of Velizh after a 4-year-old boy Fedor Emelyanov was violently murdered there in April 1823. The autopsy report of his corpse, which is found among the original case papers and was attached to the State Duma interpellation[1], is striking due to its astonishing similarity with the facts revealed in the case of Yushchinsky's murder.

Although the Jews guilty of Fedor's murder could not be identified, both the Velizh district court and the Governing Senate firmly established that it was the Jews who did this crime, for sadistic religious reasons. The State Council, where the case was submitted for final settlement, did not deny this fact either.[2]

In 1823, on the Feast of Christ's Resurrection (April 22), four-year-old Fedor, the son of Emelyan Ivanov, a private of the Velizh Invalid Detachment, went out of his home in the afternoon, did not come back and could not be found by his parents. On the Wednesday of St. Thomas's Week (May 2), the boy's dead body was found at a distance of about one mile outside Velizh, in a swamp overgrown with shrubs. At a distance of about 15 sazhens [35 meters] from the swamp, the trail of a carriage with wrought iron wheels, drawn by a pair of horses, was noticed.

Having examined the body (on May 4), the district doctor of Velizh established:

"In many places, the skin got, so to say, scorched, was yellow or red, and hardened. There were five small and round wounds on the right arm – from the hand to the elbow, both on the inner and outer sides; three similar wounds on the left arm; one similar wound on the back of the right leg above the knee; one similar wound on the back; four similar wounds on the head – on its very top and on its right side behind the ear, which have penetrated to the very bone of the skull, but

---

[1] A parliamentary question submitted in 1911 by the Russian State Duma in connection with Andrei Yushchinsky's murder. – *Translator's Note*.

[2] The following text is taken from the original case records. A more complete version can be found in *The Murder of Andrei Yushchinsky*, chapter 3.6, "The Velizh and Saratov Cases". – *Translator's Note*.

did not damage it; these wounds were almost half an inch in depth, similar to those made by large lead shot, and were inflicted, in his opinion, with a nail whose sharp end had been broken off on purpose. On both legs from the knee downwards, the skin, 1/4 arshin [18 cm] in width, differed from the rest of the skin in a dark, almost black color. The lips were tightly pressed against the teeth, and the nose against the mouth; [there was] a bloody mark of dark crimson color on the back of the neck. The stomach and the intestine were completely empty; yet, they were healthy and had no signs of putrefaction."

In the doctor's opinion, all these facts proved that:

"The child was tortured to death on purpose; he could not have been killed by lead shot; he had been fed by his parents very well (for wherever the doctor dissected him, he always found a lot of fat under the skin); he was kept on a strict diet for several days; his mouth was tied up tightly so that his screams would not be heard; he was rubbed by a cloth or a brush so as to cause a strong circulation of blood; his legs were tied up tightly so as to direct the flow of blood to the upper parts [of the body]; he was pricked, or, more exactly, his skin was pierced in 14 places in order to extract subcutaneous blood only; this misdeed was done to the undressed child, for no trace of blood was found on his shirt; and, finally, this act of barbarity had been done no earlier than two or three days before the dead body was found."[1]

[The second trial occurred in the Russian city of Saratov following the ritual murder of two boys in December 1852 and January 1853, and will be discussed at length in the next chapter. – *Translator's Note*.]

---

[1] See a detailed account of the Velizh case in *A Memorandum on Ritual Murders*, chapter "The Velizh Case". – *Translator's Note*.

Verdict of the State Council in the Case of the Murder of Two Christian Boys by the Jews in Saratov[1]

First of all, the State Council deemed it necessary to establish whether the existence or non-existence of the so-called blood doctrine among the Jews could influence the decision in the present case.

In this regard, the State Council took account of the fact that the issue of the use of Christian blood by the Jews for religious purposes or for curing diseases has been studied by theologians and other scholars for several centuries, but despite a large number of works, some of which confirm and some of which refute the existence of the said doctrine – works which still continue to appear – this issue has not yet been resolved, and therefore it cannot be taken into consideration for the purposes of making a judicial decision. Accordingly, having left aside any opinions as to the secret doctrines of the Jewish faith or its secret sects or the influence which such doctrines could have had upon the consideration of the present case by the State Council, and having considered the facts of the case exclusively, the State Council has firmly established that the existence of the crime as such, regardless of the motives for it, has been fully and undoubtedly proven here: The corpses of Feofan Sherstobitov and Mikhail Maslov, boys who had disappeared without a trace, were found shortly afterwards, with obvious signs of wounds inflicted upon Maslov while he was still alive, and with those of tortures inflicted on both boys, and – that which is most noteworthy – with obvious signs of the circumcision of their foreskins,[2] which, as it is known, is one of the fundamental rites of the Jewish religion. Therefore, all that remains is to establish the perpetrators and accomplices of, or the participants in, this crime, on the basis of their own confessions, and on that of the evidence and all the established details.

Quite a lot of persons have been charged in connection with this

---

[1] In the presence of Emperor Alexander II himself. – *I.I. Lyutostansky.*

[2] As noted by G.G. Zamyslovsky in *The Murder of Andrei Yushchinsky*, "[a]s far as Sherstobitov's corpse was concerned, it had decomposed so much that it was no longer possible to make a thorough examination of the injuries. Still, the traces of the circumcision performed on the boy were established quite definitely." – *Translator's Note.*

case. In order to establish the degree of guilt of every defendant as easily and correctly as possible, the defendants can be divided into four categories.

The first category includes those who voluntarily confessed to the crime and testified against others; these are Anton Bogdanov, a private soldier; Kryuger, a provincial secretary; and Lokotkov, an underage state [i.e., free] peasant. The second category consists of those who did not confess to the crime, but still were accused by other defendants; these are Yankel Yushkevicher, a petty bourgeois; and two private soldiers, Mikhel Shlifferman[1] and Fedor Yurlov. The third category includes defendants who caused disagreement – as far as their degree of guilt is concerned – between the Governing Senate and the ministers who considered the case. Finally, the fourth category contains all the other defendants, with regard to whom the Senate and the ministers were unanimous.

Without going into a detailed consideration of the latter category of defendants, whose degree of guilt was established without any kind of difficulty due to the clear and definite nature of both the charges brought against them and the punishment prescribed for those charges, the State Council proceeded with the discussion of the degree of guilt of, and the punishment for, the other defendants.

The State Council took account of the fact that Anton Bogdanov, a private of the Saratov garrison battalion, Avxenty Lokotkov, a state peasant, and Ivan Kryuger, a provincial secretary, voluntarily confessed during the investigation. Bogdanov confessed to being present when Sherstobitov was murdered by the Jews, and to taking the bodies of both boys from Yankel Yushkevicher's apartment to the Volga, for which he received money. Lokotkov confessed to taking the blame for Maslov's murder upon himself, following Jewish requests, and to carrying the boy's body from a barn to the Volga. Kryuger confessed to being present when Maslov was circumcised and tortured in a Jewish prayer house, and to failing to inform the authorities about it.

Although Bogdanov repeatedly changed his testimony during the investigation, he still testified against everyone who was charged with the crime, and also wrongfully accused Gubitsky, a medical assistant, but later retracted this accusation. All of this cannot undermine the reliability of Bogdanov's accusations against the others, particularly so because he did not retract these accusations in his last testimony. And if during his first interrogations Bogdanov did not give the names of all the participants in the crime and all its details, it could be explained

---

[1] Sometimes written as "Shliferman" (with one "f"). – *Translator's Note.*

partially by his confusion during the first interrogations, and partially by his having forgotten [the said names and details], because Bogdanov was interrogated for the first time when almost five months had passed since the incident. But his last testimony contains details of every kind, which he undoubtedly recalled due to questions from the judicial commission (it took the commission ten meetings to obtain this testimony alone).

As to the accusation Bogdanov had made against Gubitsky and had later retracted, it actually strongly suggests the sincerity of Bogdanov's last testimony, for he became convinced of the groundlessness of his initial accusation and no longer wanted to implicate a man whose guilt had not been confirmed during the investigation. Therefore, there are no valid reasons for *not* trusting this last testimony, which was given by Bogdanov after numerous interrogations and where, with complete remorse, he gave all the details of the manner in which the boys were murdered. Furthermore, it is quite possible that Bogdanov, who had led a vagrant's life since his childhood and had been a drunkard, could have easily been incited to the crime, all the more so because he had constantly communicated with the Jews and had been friends with the Jews from the Saratov garrison battalion, as attested to under oath by several persons of lower ranks, who said that Bogdanov had behaved "like a Jew" with the Jews.

Regardless of this, in confirmation of the testimonies given by Bogdanov, Kryuger and Lokotkov, the investigation has established:

1) the corpses of both boys showed obvious signs of circumcision; on Maslov's corpse, a wound was also found under the right shoulder, from which blood had been drawn, according to Kryuger's testimony; this fact is consistent with Bogdanov's testimony as to the torturing of Sherstobitov, whose body was not examined as thoroughly due to its utter putrefaction;

2) on the place where Maslov was tortured and blood splashed according to Kryuger's testimony, a stain was found, left by unknown persons;

3) the basement where Sherstobitov was tortured had indeed been rented by Yankel Yushkevicher according to the testimonies of several persons questioned in the case;

4) the removal of an object covered with a sheepskin coat [on a sledge], by the Jews, from the house where Yushkevicher lived, is consistent with the manner in which Maslov's corpse had been removed according to Bogdanov, and is also corroborated by [other] witness testimonies; and

5) Lokotkov did state, in the 1st Police Precinct of Saratov, that he

murdered Maslov, whose corpse had been found on the Volga; and as he was kept in custody, privates Yurlov and Shlifferman (whom Lokotkov accused of having persuaded him to do so) did come to him at night.

Thus, it has been established that the confessions made by Bogdanov, Lokotkov and Kryuger are fully corroborated by the facts of the case, and this proves beyond doubt that Bogdanov and Lokotkov had concealed the murder of the two boys in Saratov, while Kryuger had been present when this crime had been committed and had failed to inform the authorities about it.

As the State Council proceeded to examine the accusations made against the Saratov Jews, Yankel Yushkevicher, a petty bourgeois, and Mikhail Shlifferman, a private soldier, and against the baptized Jew, Fedor Yurlov, also a private soldier, it took account of the fact that these persons were accused by Bogdanov, Lokotkov and Kryuger of actually committing the murder of the boys. The accusers stated that Yushkevicher and Shlifferman were the main culprits in the crime, with the direct participation of Yurlov.

During numerous interrogations conducted as part of the investigation of this case, Yushkevicher, Shlifferman and Yurlov did not confess to anything and persisted in denying the accusations; and although the testimonies of their accusers (persons of blameworthy behavior and, moreover, involved in the case) cannot have the probative value required by the law, it still should be noted that the trustworthiness of their testimonies is confirmed both by the facts discovered in the case and by the fact that all the accusers, without being suspected in the least of the crime, voluntarily came to the investigator and showed remorse, and, as can be seen from the case materials, had no reason whatsoever to slander the Jews.

But regardless of these accusations made against the said defendants, the investigation discovered very numerous and important pieces of evidence, namely:

a) Against Yushkevicher:

1) Popova, a petty bourgeois, testified under oath that shortly before the Maslenitsa[1] of 1853, as she was in her room, she heard a child's sorrowful cry coming from Yushkevicher's apartment next door: "Let me go, my daddy will give you some money instead."

2) Bogdanov's statement that Yushkevicher cut a finger on his left hand when he tortured Sherstobitov was confirmed during the

---

[1] A feast, also known as Butter Week, which is celebrated the seventh week before Easter. – *Translator's Note*.

investigation by the fact that Yushkevicher, indeed, had a scar on the fourth finger of his left hand. At first, Yushkevicher would claim that this scar was caused by a pike biting him, and when a doctor established that the scar was caused by a different reason, namely by a cut with a sharp object, one made much earlier than the date given by Yushkevicher, the latter, while maintaining that he actually could have cut himself with a knife, continued to insist that he had cut his finger no earlier than one month before he was examined by the doctor.

3) Another of Bogdanov's statements, concerning the removal of Maslov's corpse from Yushkevicher's apartment, was confirmed during the investigation by the fact that a peasant named Kadomtsev saw how, shortly before the 1853 Maslenitsa, the Jews removed an object covered with a sheepskin coat, which looked like a human body, on a sledge driven by a horse of Kadomtsev's boss, Gilgenberg, a [German] colonist, while three witnesses confirmed under oath that Gilgenberg told Kadomtsev to fetch that horse to the Jews.

4) According to yet another of Bogdanov's statements, Sherstobitov was tortured in a basement which belonged to Gilgenberg. Although Gilgenberg did not confess to renting the basement to the Jews, two witnesses did attest to it: one testified that he heard from Gilgenberg that the basement was rented to Yushkevicher; and another said that, shortly before the Maslenitsa of that year, he saw Yushkevicher and his wife taking the keys to that basement from the cupboard of the hotel kept by Gilgenberg.

5) As testified under oath by several persons, during the Great Fast of that year, when Bogdanov was told to pay for the dishes he had broken in Gilgenberg's hotel, he said that Yushkevicher would do that, and shortly afterwards Yushkevicher's son did actually pay for the broken dishes.

6) Gorokhova, a petty bourgeois, testified that she heard from Yushkevicher's wife that the boys were circumcised, tortured and murdered in a Jewish prayer house, and that Yushkevicher received a large amount of money from the Volhynia province for the blood of those boys, which was needed for Jewish religious rites.

7) Regarding the meaning of the words in an intercepted letter by Yushkevicher, written on a piece of paper with a burnt splinter, namely, "Tell the Jews to pray. You all must stand firm. Be strong, my dear daughter, that is what I ask from you and your brother", Yushkevicher could not provide a trustworthy justification.

8) Regarding Lokotkov's testimony that Yushkevicher persuaded him to take the blame for the murder upon himself, when they both were held in prison, Yushkevicher did not confess to it and claimed that

he did not even know Lokotkov; however, this claim was disproved by two witnesses who saw how Yushkevicher and Lokotkov spoke to each other in hushed tones.

9) Yushkevicher's son-in-law, a Jew named Mordukh Guglin (Nikolai Petrov after Holy Baptism), testified that his father-in-law repeatedly confessed to murdering the boys before him, and that when Yushkevicher was held in jail, he (Yushkevicher) asked him (Guglin) to destroy a suspicious letter kept by Yushkevicher's daughter, where two bottles of blood sealed with red and black wax, which were to be sent to the Lyubavichi rabbi, were mentioned.

b) Against Shlifferman:

1) When Shlifferman, together with 43 other privates, was showed to a boy named Kanin, the latter recognized Shlifferman to be the man who had decoyed Maslov.

2) According to Shlifferman's own confession, he alone performed circumcisions on the Jews in Saratov.

3) Shlifferman's statement that he did not even know Lokotkov was disproven by the sworn testimonies of two persons, who saw Shlifferman visiting Lokotkov on the day of the latter's arrest.

4) According to Gorokhova's testimony, she heard from Yushkevicher's wife that it was Shlifferman who kidnapped the boys, and that Yushkevicher received a large amount of money from the Volhynia province for the blood of those boys.

c) Against Yurlov:

1) According to Gorokhova's testimony, when Yurlov learned from her about Yushkevicher's arrest, he started crying and said: "It is our sin, we are all doomed now;" and when Gorokhova asked him who participated in the murder, Yurlov replied: "You know it yourself – those who were arrested, they did."

2) Yurlov's confession to the murder of the boys was also attested to by Mordukh Guglin (Nikolai Petrov).

3) Yurlov's statement that he had not known Bogdanov until he was enrolled in the army, and that he did not know Lokotkov at all proved to be false during the investigation.

The totality of the above-mentioned pieces of evidence, directly related to the circumcision, torturing and murder of the boys and leaving not the slightest doubt as to the guilt of Yushkevicher, Shlifferman and Yurlov, is absolute proof that they did commit the crime in question.

As the State Council then proceeded to examine the accusations made against the defendants who caused disagreement between the Governing Senate and the ministers who considered the case, namely the Jews Itska Berlinsky, Ezdra Zaydman and Yankel Berman, it established that there is evidence in the case which arouses suspicion as to their participation in the murder together with the main culprits, namely: the accusation that they participated in the crime, made against all of them by Bogdanov and Kryuger; their false testimonies during the investigation; and, furthermore, a piece of printed calico found in Berlinsky's apartment, which was similar to the cloth of the shirt worn by Sherstobitov prior to his disappearance.

Finally, the State Council could not help but pay attention to the fact that Bogdanov and Lokotkov, as guilty of concealing the murders, and Kryuger, as guilty of failing to report the crime, are supposed to be subjected to quite harsh punishment in accordance with the law, namely: Bogdanov and Lokotkov are supposed to be attainted and sentenced to hard labor, while Kryuger is supposed to be exiled to the Vyatka province. However, all these persons sincerely repented having participated in the crime and thereby revealed the main culprits in this major case. Taking this fact into account, the State Council, on its part, in agreement with the opinion of the military minister, found it possible to ask the Emperor to mitigate the punishment for the said defendants.

Hereupon, considering that failure to punish the main culprits only because they strongly persisted in denying the charges would be totally against the demands of justice, the State Council has ruled that:

1) the Jew Yankel Yushkevicher, a petty bourgeois, the Jew Mikhail Shlifferman, a private of the Saratov garrison battalion, and the baptized Jew Fedor Yurlov, a private of the same battalion, for the murder of two Christian boys in the town of Saratov by torturing and tormenting them, are to be attainted and sentenced to hard labor in mines: Yushkevicher and Shlifferman, for 20 years each, and Yurlov, for 18 years, exempting them from corporal punishment by virtue of a Most Gracious Imperial Manifest;

2) Anton Bogdanov, a private of the Saratov garrison battalion, Avxenty Lokotkov, a state peasant, and Ivan Kryuger, a retired provincial secretary, guilty: the former two, of concealing the crime in question, and the latter, of failing to inform the authorities about it, are to be brought to the Monarch's attention, so that His Imperial Highness, if He wished so, taking into account the open-hearted confession of these defendants, owing to which the main culprits in the present case were revealed, would rule as follows: Bogdanov is to be sent to a detention company of the engineer department for two years in order to correct his behavior; Lokotkov is to be confined to a workhouse for the same period of time; and Kryuger, without depriving him of the rights and privileges he acquired during his service, is to be exiled to one of

the remote provinces, at the discretion of the Minister of Internal Affairs, and subjected there to strict police supervision, and, furthermore, for his liaison with Beloshapchenkova, a provincial secretary, penance is to be imposed on him, at the discretion of the ecclesiastical authorities;

3) Itska Berlinsky, a private of the Balashov Invalid Detachment, Ezdra Zaydman, a private of a coast guard unit, and Yankel Berman, a private of the Saratov Invalid Detachment, are to be left under suspicion[1] for their participation, together with the culprits, in the murder of two Christian boys in the town of Saratov, and in accordance with the Imperial Decree announced in the order for the military department, are to be exiled to Siberia; as to the rest of the defendants, the unanimous opinion of the Governing Senate and the ministers who considered the present case is to be approved.[2]

As we now conclude the detailed account of the Saratov case, we would like to remind the readers what we said in the preface to this book: We do not impose our opinion on the subject in question upon the readers, but rather we limit our modest role to assembling historical and legal facts and documents. By an impartial study of these, the readers should draw their own conclusions, and we, on our part, would be happy if our work allows them to draw such conclusions after a critical examination of the materials included herein.

In 1901, a similar case happened in Saint Petersburg itself, where only educated and selected Jews live. A laundress brought her 2-year-old daughter to the Yusupov garden, left her there with the children of a woman of her acquaintance, and went off on some errand.

Half an hour later, she returned to the garden where she had left her child, but could not find it among the children. The woman with whom she had left her child told her that it was probably taken away by a Jewish woman who had been sitting near the child, caressing it; then, the Jewish woman had disappeared, and so did the child. The mother

---

[1] In those days, "leaving under suspicion" was a legal term which meant something between conviction and acquittal. – *Translator's Note.*

[2] More information about the Saratov case can be found in *The Murder of Andrei Yushchinsky*, chapter 3.6, "The Velizh and Saratov Cases". – *Translator's Note.*

went searching for her daughter, informed the police, announcements were published in newspapers, but the missing child was not to be found anywhere.

Three days after the disappearance of the girl, a neighbor came to the broken-hearted mother to borrow a tub so as to wash the laundry. The mother told her to go to the shed and take the tub from there. The neighbor did so and found the tub lying upside-down in the shed. She turned the tub over and discovered the corpse of [the missing] child underneath. It was pricked all over, with no clean spot to be seen on it.

The police took the body to the Alexandrovskaya hospital, put it into the mortuary, and a lot of people would examine it. An investigation was carried out, but nothing was established, and the body was eventually buried.

Hundreds of cases were dismissed in this manner, being committed "to God's will" because the culprits could not be discovered, despite the Jews being suspected.

The records of proceedings and the case papers are kept in the 4th Spassky Precinct (St. Petersburg, Troitsky Ave., 10), and there are still a lot of witnesses. I.A. Sergeyev along with his wife and many of his workers can give eyewitness accounts of this case.

It should be stressed that the barbaric custom of using Christian blood exists among the Talmudic Jews only (the Talmudists, not the Karaites).

On September 25, a group of parents informed the Saint Petersburg police about the disappearance of the following children: Alexandra Nikolayeva, 8 years of age; Afanasiya Filippova, 13 years of age; Timofey Andreyev, 13 years of age; a boy named Nikolai, 7 or 8 years of age (clad in a brown jacket); and Shura Nikolayeva, 7 years of age (clad in a white-and-red blouse).

Every year, 15 to 20 children disappear in Saint Petersburg, as attested to by the municipal authorities. Polish Jews come to Russia in winter in order to kidnap Christian children, and they freely draw their blood in large cities due to the ignorance of the Russian people, who do not believe that the Jews use Christian blood.

An Anxious Easter in Sofia

Several years ago, the Easter celebration in Sofia, the Bulgarian capital, was held during a period of very great local anxiety. It was feared that the populace might have revolted against the local Jews and lynched them at any time, but a terrible pogrom was avoided by strict measures taken in due time by the authorities. Still, the Christian population were not completely pacified, impatiently awaiting the results of the judicial investigation. The anxiety had been caused by the following incident: During Holy Week, two Jewish junk dealers tried to kidnap two young girls (daughters of General Velchev and a lawyer named Tolev) while they were playing on the street. Toleva managed to break away from the kidnappers, but Yelena Velcheva was taken away by the Jews, who gagged her with a kerchief to keep her from screaming. Fortunately, as they carried their burden, the kidnappers were noticed by two constables, who immediately freed the girl and arrested the Jews.

News of this mysterious incident, which coincided (perhaps, completely by chance) with Holy Week, spread throughout the city with the speed of lightning, and it was only thanks to urgent military and police measures that a most terrifying Jewish pogrom was prevented – so violent was the agitation of the Christian population of Sofia, which ascribed ritual motives to this crime. In addition to the military and police measures, it was the most influential part of the local press that greatly contributed to preventing a pogrom with its reasonable advice, persuasion, and appeal to confide in the judicial authorities which were trying to establish the true purpose of this outrageous crime.[1]

Generally, because of its ignorance, the Bulgarian press refuses to accept the popular belief about the existence of secret rites within the Jewish religion, and tries to associate this crime with other motives, appealing to the Jewish population of the Bulgarian capital – in order to remove any suspicion on the part of their Christian fellow citizens – to renounce once and for all the traditional secluded way of their religious and family life, which is the main reason why Christians believe in the existence of Jewish religious murders. This kind of press – which

---

[1] Some of this text was apparently quoted from a Bulgarian newspaper. – *Translator's Note.*

defends and helps the Jews for money, just like the police – has always existed, everywhere, as seen from the Abramova case, which occurred last year in Smolensk shortly before Easter.

Fanatical Jewish Policy Against Christians

For almost 2,000 years, Jewry has been trying – either secretly or, if possible, openly – to exterminate Christians with every possible means. More recently, it has become much easier for the Jews to destroy the *Goim* in all their ways. They incite Christians to rebellion, causing them to slaughter each other, while the Jews, rubbing their hands with joy, laugh gleefully. They have seized control of the medical profession and drugstores, so Christian lives are now in Jewish hands. Thus, the Jews could, if they wished, kill hundreds of thousands of Christians in a single day. Jewish doctors give detailed advice on the performance of abortions. Finally, in Russia, in all the regions inhabited by the Jews, scores of small children disappear. They are kidnapped partly for ritual needs, as evidenced by the facts; however, sometimes the Jews kill children for no special reason, tying stones to their necks and throwing them into water. In a word, they try to decrease the Christian population while increasing their own, so as to take possession of the Christian world.

Let us make some brief quotations from the Talmud. The Russian people should pay particular attention to the book of *Shulchan Aruch*, and the treatises *Iore Dea* (158, 1, *Hagah*) and *Abodah Zarah* (26). A Jew is not compelled to kill an *Akum* (a *Goi*, a Russian) with whom he lives in peace, but, at the same time, he is strongly forbidden to save this *Akum* from death if, for instance, the latter falls into water, even if he promised the Jew all his property for saving him. Next, a Jewish doctor is forbidden to treat an *Akum*, even for money, unless failure to do so would cause anti-Jewish hatred among the *Akum*. In this case, a Jew is even allowed to treat an *Akum* for free. Also, a Jew is permitted to test a medicine on the *Akum* to see whether it brings about a cure or causes death, etc. etc. Those wishing further details may consult the second volume of our work *The Talmud and The Jews*.

Saint Gavriil (Gabriel of Bialystok)

"Saint Gavriil, whose relics repose in the Slutsky Holy Trinity Orthodox Monastery near the town of Slutsk, the district capital, was born, according to the monastery's records, in 1684 in the village of Zverki, near the town of Zabludov, and in 1690 he was kidnapped in Bely Stan [Belostok, Bialystok] by a Jewish leaseholder from the same village, tortured to death and thrown away in a field to be eaten by birds. Gavriil's parents found his body and buried it in the Zabludov Orthodox Monastery. Thirty years later, Saint Gavriil's remains were exhumed and placed in a church vault. On May 9, 1755, [the remains] were moved from Zabludov to the Slutsky Holy Trinity Monastery by the Monastery's archimandrite Mikhail Kazachinsky."[1]

Almost the same information about Saint Gavriil is provided by *History of the Russian Hierarchy* (Moscow, 1815, vol. 6, p. 148): "The Slutsky Holy Trinity Men's Monastery of the Minsk Eparchy is situated on the shore of the Sluch River, half a mile from Slutsk, the district capital. The monastery had seven churches, and now it has three. One of them, made of stone, the Church of the Holy Trinity, has two side chapels; Saint Gavriil's imperishable relics repose there. As seen from the monastery's records, he was born in 1684 in the village of Zverki, near the town of Zabludov, and in 1690 he was kidnapped in Bely Stan by a Jewish leaseholder from the same village and tortured to death. When his parents found his body, which had been thrown away in a field to be eaten by birds, they buried it, after a [forensic] examination, in the Zabludov Orthodox Monastery, now situated in the Belostok province. Thirty years later, when another [body] was buried, [Saint Gavriil's] body was exhumed intact and placed in a church vault. On May 9, 1755, [the remains] were moved from the Zabludov Orthodox Monastery to the Slutsky Holy Trinity Monastery by the former archimandrite of Slutsk, Mikhail Kazachinsky."

"Saint Gavriil's relics are the main sacred object of the Monastery. They openly repose in a small wooden coffin. The hands clasp a small metallic communion cross; the fingers are pricked all over, and there are lacerated wounds on the flesh; the fingernails are intact; and the

---

[1] *Historical Dictionary of Saints Glorified by the Russian Church...*, St. Petersburg, 1836. – *I.I. Lyutostansky*.

head is separated from the body. No hagiography of Saint Gavriil still exists. The memory of Saint Gavriil is celebrated by the Christian Orthodox Church on April 20, the day of his martyrdom. Above the reliquary, set in a frame under glass is the biography of this martyr, which says: '**Headstone.** Of Gavriil Gavdelyuchenko, a baby from the village of Zverki, Zabludov county, born on March 22, 1684 and tortured to death by the Jews in Bely Stok on April 20, 1690. Those who want to learn more about it are referred to the Magdeburg legal codes of Zabludov. His holy relics were moved from Zabludov to the Slutsky Archimandrite Monastery on May 9, 1775, during the happy rule of the Most Excellent Prince Hieronim Radziwill.' "[1]

The biography is followed by a poem describing the torments of this holy martyr.[2]

The text of the divine service for Saint Gavriil was written by Metropolitan Antony, Archbishop of Volhynia, in 1908, who printed it and brought it to Saint Petersburg. His Eminence stopped in the Alexander Nevsky Lavra and sent me a copy as a gift, with his visiting card. On the next day, I brought him the two volumes of my book *On the Use of Christian Blood by the Jews*.

---

[1] F.F. Serno-Solovyevich, *The Ancient Russian Town of Slutsk and Its Sacred Objects*, Vilna, 1886. – *Translator's Note*.

[2] As already mentioned, Saint Gavriil's relics are currently kept in Saint Nicholas' Cathedral in Bialystok, Poland. His memory is still celebrated by the Christian Orthodox Church. In August 2012, Patriarch Kirill of Moscow, head of the Russian Orthodox Church, as he was on a visit to Poland, paid homage to Saint Gavriil's relics. – *Translator's Note*.

Other Monuments to Children Murdered by the Jews

In the memorial book of the Vilna province for 1860 (part 2, article on the Jews, p. 39), it says in an addendum:
"In the St. Bernardine Roman Catholic Church of Vilna, a monument still stands, bearing a similar inscription[1] about a baby murdered by the Jews."

We personally visited this monument in Vilna. Near the entrance to the St. Bernardine Church, in a wall recess on its left, there is a small marble coffin, with an inscription in Latin underneath. The inscription (see below) says that the body of a 7-year-old child named Simon Kierelis, a native of Vilna, barbarically murdered by the Jews in 1592 A.D., is buried there.

> D. T. O. M. D.
> **Memoria**
> Sugenui pueri Simonis Kierelis natione Vilnen.
> Septimo aetatis anno crudelissime a Judeis Vulneribus centrum septua ginta accisi in angulo hujus ecclesia tumulati.
> Anno a Christi nato 1592.
> **Erecta**
> Ex. Elemosinis Benefactorum

In *Obrazy z zycia i podrozy* by J.I. Kraszewski (1842, vol. 1), we find a description of the town of Kodnia above the Bug River. On p. 60, it says: "In a local church, there is a monument of a baby murdered by the Jews. Many such monuments may be found in various places."

On p. 61 of the same book, we find the story of this baby:
"A 3-year-old boy Maciej (Mathias), on May 8, 1698, on the last day of the Feast of the Cross, when everybody was participating in the icon-bearing procession, remained home alone. As he became tired of waiting for the return of his family, he went into a field. There, he was caught by the Jews, who secretly murdered him in their house and

---

[1] Similar to the inscription about Saint Gavriil. – *Translator's Note.*

Other Monuments to Children Murdered by the Jews

abandoned the body in a forest. His body was found by a shepherd's dog in the forest, brought to Kodnia and placed in the town hall. After an investigation, the baby's murderers were identified and publicly beheaded in a marketplace. The synagogue was destroyed, and most of the Jews were expelled from the town. The body of the murdered baby was buried in a church with great solemnity, and a monument was erected at his grave with a moving inscription [see below]."

> Atrox non atrum – Amaeno vultu lege fatum Viator. Codnae ignobili ortum Lucina trianulum Mathiam de lustrali fonte, nobilitavit exitu; coeca Judeorum perfidia, immortali groliae prospexit: Purpuratum aeternis initiavit annis, cruenta coede, etc. etc. etc. Quae repetitam in Mathiae sanguine Christi necem alta *duorum Judeorum croure fuso*, stilit fideles lachrymas, reposuit inhumatae innocentiae monumentum impietas, sublato Synagogae fano etc. A 1698 die 10 Maij.
> – Monument erected in 1713.

In the city of Grodno, in a local Catholic church, there is a stone monument in Polish which says that a 6-year-old Christian girl went missing and that her corpse was later found in a field, pricked all over. Her parents buried the body, and everyone was fully convinced that the girl was murdered by Jewish fanatics. The monument is in poor condition, so the year of its erection is illegible.

We could mention a lot of other monuments of this kind, but it would tire the reader, so we will stop here.

Charters of Immunity Mentioning Ritual Murders

Since the authors of certain legal documents (see below) found it necessary to mention this barbaric Jewish custom on various occasions, one could hardly doubt its existence.

Thus, in Article 9 of the charter of immunity issued by Prince Boleslaw and approved by Casimir the Great and Witold of Lithuania, it says that when a Jew is accused of murdering a Christian baby, three witnesses, both Christian and Jewish, must be produced; and if the accuser does not prove this accusation, he must be subjected himself to the punishment prescribed for this kind of crime.

In the 16th century, the Polish-Lithuanian authorities, due to their complete financial dependence on the Jews, started protecting the Jews from persecution by the indignant Christian population. We have detailed information about the trials which had given rise to the prosecution.[1]

In 1564, King Sigismund Augustus, in issuing a charter of immunity to Lithuanian Jews to protect them from accusations of murdering Christian children, briefly mentioned that he had been impelled to do so by acts of violence committed against the Jews in the town of Bielsk, whose residents had suspected a Jew of murdering a Christian child. Claiming that this fact had not been proven and that the accusation in itself was incompatible with the actual beliefs and rites of the Jews, the king, in order to protect the Jews in similar situations, ruled that that such cases were to be removed from the competence of ordinary courts and were to be considered by the king's court exclusively.

The decree further says that the accused persons were not to be taken into custody, but were to be released on bail of two local or neighboring Jewish residents. And it was only in the absence of bailsmen that the defendant could be detained; still, he or she was not to be put into irons, but was to be kept under good conditions.

The crime was only to be considered proven if seven witnesses testified against the culprit: four settled Christians of good behavior, and three Jews, also of exemplary behavior. If the defendant was

---

[1] See *Documents of the Vilna Archeographic Commission*, vol. 5, p. 88. – *I.I. Lyutostansky*.

acquitted, the accuser was to be sentenced to the execution prescribed for the crime in question.[1]

Obviously, not only did such strict requirements protect the Jews against false denunciations, they also allowed them to go unpunished even if they *were* guilty.

Yet, very shortly afterwards, the Jews were accused of a similar crime in the village of Rososz [Rosoch], Brest [Brzesc] starostwo [crown land]. Again, the Jews were fully acquitted, and another charter of immunity was issued in 1566, which confirmed the previous one.[2] In 1576, King Stefan issued yet another charter of immunity.[3]

Now, the second charter issued by Sigismund Augustus is of interest to us because it describes the [1566] Rososz case, albeit briefly and in a very pro-Jewish manner.[4]

It should be mentioned that the investigation was carried out by Ostaf Wollowicz, Lithuanian sub-chancellor and royal court counselor, in his capacity of Brest starosta [head of the community], while the Jewish defendant, Nachim, was in the service of the main tax collector, Izaak Brodawka, the very person who had been accused of the Bielsk murder [in 1564], and who, together with Wollowicz, was a member of the tax collection commission.

Many residents of Rososz of both sexes testified that they had seen Nachim, while riding on horseback from Horodyszcze, grab a child walking along the road to its mother in the fields, and ride away with it. An investigation was initiated, and after the examination of Nachim's horse and the tracks on the road from Horodyszcze, it was firmly established that it was Nachim who had been seen on the road. His horse had been shod on one foot only, just like the kidnapper's horse. Nachim was brought to trial, and in accordance with the above-mentioned charter of Sigismund Augustus, he was released on bail of as many as twelve Jews from Rososz.

Meanwhile, the child's corpse was found and examined by the court. Unfortunately, the very important report of this examination has not been preserved.

People started talking that, according to many accounts, a Jewish girl named Lichanka related that Nachim brought this child to their

---

[1] *Papers of the Vladimir Court*, 1567, no. 934, sheet 27; *Charters of Great Lithuanian Princes*, p. 97; *Documents of the Vilna Archeographic Commission*, vol. 5, p. 217. – *I.I. Lyutostansky.*

[2] *Ibid.* – *I.I. Lyutostansky.*

[3] *Documents of the Vilna Archeographic Commission*, vol. 5, p. 214. – *I.I. Lyutostansky.*

[4] *Charters of Great Lithuanian Princes*, p. 110. – *I.I. Lyutostansky.*

house, kept it there for three days, feeding it with pies and giving it vodka and mead to drink, and then, together with another Jew, Rabey, cut it to death at night. Lichanka's brother, Itska, held the child's arms. Lichanka got very frightened thinking her little brother, Zelka, was being murdered. After the child was cut to death, the murderers skinned the corpse, removed the heart and licked it; according to other accounts, the heart was fried and eaten by them. As she was interrogated, Lichanka denied that she had ever said that, and the case was dismissed due to lack of evidence.

The Vilna Case of Vintsenta Grudzinskaya, Whose Blood Was Drawn by the Jews

In 1900, in the early hours of March 2, in the apartment of David Blondes, a Jewish barber, an attempted murder of Vintsenta Grudzinskaya, a young Christian girl, took place. Several days earlier, two days before Passover, Grudzinskaya had been hired by Blondes as a maidservant. On the evening before the incident, Blondes asked her to go to bed early, saying that she would have to wake up early in the morning and do some work.

The case was heard by a jury in the Vilna District Court from December 15 to 21, 1900, and produced a strong effect not only in Lithuania, but also far beyond its borders.

The facts of the case were as follows: In the early hours of March 2, at 2:30 a.m., a young girl was brought by a policeman to the 3rd Police Precinct in a cab. She had two very fresh wounds on her neck and left arm. When the precinct superintendent asked her who had inflicted these wounds and under what circumstances, she said that the Jews had wanted to cut her to death, namely David Blondes, a barber whom she served, and another Jew.

When asked about the motives for it, she answered she did not know. However, street cleaners who were present there all said that the Jews had probably wanted to get some blood for their Passover matzo, all the more so because the Jewish feast of Purim was to begin on March 2.

Grudzinskaya briefly told the superintendent that about 2 a.m., as she was working in Blondes' kitchen, two Jews suddenly rushed in from Blondes' room and assaulted her. White kerchiefs covered their faces, with only slits for their eyes. One of the Jews grabbed her by the head, while the other cut her throat and left arm with a knife or blade. Right at that moment, a loud noise came from the street, causing great confusion among the Jews. Seizing this opportunity, Grudzinskaya broke away from her assailants and ran out into the street, where local street cleaners and a policeman named Belik took her under their protection.

As Grudzinskaya needed urgent medical help, the superintendent ordered her to be taken to the Savich hospital. On the basis of her statement, an investigation was launched on the same day, March 2.

As Grudzinskaya was examined by a doctor, a transverse wound 4.5 cm in length was found on the left of her neck, a wound which reached the cartilage. For a length of 2 cm, this wound was directed towards the ear, where the carotid artery was located. The wound on the left arm, also 4.5 cm in length, had been made with a sharp cutting tool.

As she was questioned as a victim, Grudzinskaya confirmed her previous testimony.

Next, on the basis of witness testimonies, it was established that in the early hours of March 2, at two o'clock sharp, two cabmen, as they were driving on Tatarskaya Street, came upon a small wooden bridge at a distance of several steps from David Blondes' barber's shop. Suddenly, one end of the bridge collapsed under their wheels, while the other lifted up and then fell down, making a loud noise which resounded throughout the street. At that moment, the city clock struck two. Several moments later, the front door of Blondes' apartment thrust open, and Vintsenta Grudzinskaya ran out into the street from the apartment, barefoot, with an uncovered head, and clad only in a thin blouse.

After running a certain distance, she rang at the gate of Kulesh's house, where her cousin, Adam Grudzinsky, worked as a street cleaner. As he opened the gate, Adam saw that Vintsenta was stained with blood and trembling all over. He asked her what happened. At first, Vintsenta, overwhelmed with fear, would not answer, but then, as she entered Adam's apartment, she sat down, utterly exhausted, and said with effort: "Poor me, the Jews wanted to cut me to death." She had fresh wounds on her neck and her left arm, with blood pouring from them.

Adam ran to the nearest police post and reported the incident to Belik, the policeman, who immediately took the necessary measures.

After she calmed down a bit, Vintsenta told Adam and his wife that as she was washing the table in Blondes' kitchen, two men assaulted her. She recognized one of them (the shorter one) as her boss, Blondes. He cut her neck with a knife, and then wounded her arm. It was only thanks to a loud noise from the street, frightening her assailants, that she managed to break away from them and run out into the street.

She could not explain why the Jews inflicted wounds on her, but she suspected they did so because they wanted to get Christian blood. One of the reasons for this conclusion was the fact that a Jewish bakery stood in Blondes' courtyard.

The case was heard in public court from December 15 to 21, 1900. The following questions were submitted to the jurors:

1) Has it been proved that on the night of March 2, 1900, in the city of Vilna, on Tatarskaya Street, in the house of the reformatory synod, in the apartment of David Abramovich Blondes, a petty bourgeois from Vilna, two wounds were inflicted to the neck and left arm of a peasant named Vintsenta Grudzinskaya, with a sharp cutting tool?

2) If the criminal act described in question no. 1 has been proven, then is David Abramovich Blondes, a 32-year-old petty bourgeois from Vilna, guilty of the following: at the hour and place specified in question no. 1, having agreed in advance with another person, not identified by the investigation, and together with this person, having a deliberate intent to kill Vintsenta Grudzinskaya, he inflicted two wounds on her, to her neck and left arm, with a sharp cutting tool, but was unable to fulfill the said intent for reasons out of his control, because he was frightened by a noise from the street, and consequently had to leave Grudzinskaya?

3) Is Blondes guilty of inflicting the wounds on Vintsenta Grudzinskaya, under the same circumstances, in a state of excitement and irritation?

The jurors found that the fact of the crime and Blondes' guilt, as described in question no. 2, had been proved, in the following wording: "Yes, he is guilty, but he had no intent to kill". Question no. 3 was left unanswered by them.

The district court found that Article 1482 of the Criminal Code was to be applied to Blondes' crime, as established by the decision of the jurors, and, in accordance with this article, the punishment was to be reduced by one degree, due to the defendant's ignorance. Consequently, the court ruled that Blondes was to be deprived of all his rights and privileges and sentenced to 1 year and 4 months in prison.

In 1899 and 1900, the trials of a Jew named Leopold Hilsner took place in the town of Polna in Bohemia, Austro-Hungary. Hilsner was accused of murdering two young Christian girls by drawing their blood. He was sentenced to death. The people revolted against the Jews, but the latter collected a large amount of money, and the authorities sided with them. Eventually, the sentence was commuted to life imprisonment. Nevertheless, Hilsner was not acquitted, so the people proved to be stronger than all the judges.[1]

In Russia, hundreds of similar accusations were proven in court.

---

[1] This paragraph has been heavily edited for clarity. – *Translator's Note.*

On the Russian Names for the Jews

Translator's Note: Earlier, the Jews were called *zhidy* in Russia. However, by the end of the 19th century, this term was dismissed as offensive and replaced with *yevrei*. In this short chapter, I.I. Lyutostansky argues that this practice is completely wrong and the Jews should still be called *zhidy*. (The best analogy in English would probably be "Negro" vs. "African American".) Most of this chapter would not be interesting to the English speaker, so only its final part has been included herein.

[...] Nowhere in the world are the Jews (*zhidy*) called *yevrei*. It is only in Russia that this latter name was introduced, due to the intrigues of the Jews, who wanted to conceal their true name in order to ennoble their nation. But no matter how hard the Jews try to change their name or origin, it would not help them. Unless they change their nature and predatory manners, they would still be alien elements, hated and persecuted everywhere. During the last 4,000 years, the Jews have spread all over the world, and nowhere did they gain love, nowhere could they live with other nations as brothers. They had their own state, but could enter into alliance with no one, with no neighboring king. From the very beginning of their nomadic life, they have been notorious everywhere for their barbarity, rapaciousness and treachery; and this is what we see even today – in the danger they pose with their political intrigues, in their constant craving for Christian blood, and in their hatred towards Christians in general.

Favid (Favus), a Caste Disease of the Jews

Almost every Jew suffers from his or her "national" disease called favid (favus), and despite the performance of incessant ablutions, the Jews are surrounded by a foul and stupefying smell which makes it very unpleasant to speak with them at close range. The characteristic Jewish smell – is this a prejudice or not? A pure-blooded Jew smells of bedbugs, says Dr. [Jean-Christian] Boudin, the former president of the Anthropological Society [of Paris].

The characteristic disease of the Jewish nation, which affects almost every poor Jew, is the well-known favid. Its biblical name is "minor leprosy", while in Hebrew it is called *zarchat*. This Egyptian disease still exists in India, China and Central Asia, and is extremely contagious, painful and incurable in those places due to the hot climate. This is the main reason for the Jewish migration to the north – there, this caste disease becomes less painful and temporarily disappears.

In our country, this disease only exists among the Jews, although Christian children who come into contact with the Jews often get infected with favid as well, and then transmit it to adults. Favid can be quickly cured, but only in the case of non-Jews. As to the Jews, they cannot be cured completely of their intrinsic, native disease, which is a kind of emblem and seal of God's chosen people.

The national Jewish disease, favid, is still raging among them, as evidenced by the following news report from Vilna, published in the *Voskhod* magazine (December 2, 1899):

"Our Lithuanian Jerusalem has so many pressing needs... One of them is the establishment of a favusorium, that is, of a hospital for those suffering from one of the most unpleasant skin diseases called favus or favid. Doctors specializing in skin diseases are astonished at the growing number of cases of this disease among the Vilna Jews, a disease which is quite contagious to boot. Local doctors estimate that 300 to 400 people suffer from it (according to some data, this number is about 1,000). This disease rages among the Jews exclusively. Thus, one doctor recently informed the author of this report that 4 of 19 Jewish prostitutes examined [by him] suffered from favid, while in the case of 79 non-Jewish prostitutes this number was zero. Therefore, the establishment of a specialized hospital is a necessity for our society."

So what should be our attitude towards the Jewish nation which suffers from this contagious disease? All educational institutions are full of Jews, and they are not examined by doctors, which means that every Russian could be infected. There is a rule strictly observed in every educational institution: those who enter it must produce a certificate that they were inoculated against smallpox. However, favid is more dangerous than smallpox, because smallpox is a periodic disease, while favid is a permanent one.

Not only in Russia do the Jews suffer from their national disease; they do so everywhere, including in the USA, as it can be seen from an incident with Milyukov, a member of the [Russian] State Duma. Milyukov went to the USA as part of a delegation of Russian Jews. The American Jews met him as if he were the long-awaited Messiah. A huge crowd surrounded him, and everyone eagerly shook both his hands. On the next day, Milyukov found pimples and swelling on his fingers. As a result, he was compelled to appear in public in gloves, so that nobody would see he had favus.

This is where Milyukov's liking for the Jews brought him; he was infected with favid, so he is now of the same blood with them.[1]

---

[1] Taken from various newspapers. – *I.I. Lyutostansky*.

A Jewish Murder in Kiev[1]

On March 12, 1911 Andrei Yushchinsky, a student at the Saint Sophia Theological School in Kiev, left home for school at 6:00 o'clock in the morning after a breakfast of cold borscht. The victim lived with his mother in the district of Nikolskaya Slobodka behind the Dnieper River, at about 6 miles from the Saint Sophia Theological School in Kiev. He never reached the school and never came home. He was reported missing on March 12. Yushchinsky's corpse was found on March 20 in a small cave near Kirillovskaya Street, next to Berner's estate.

This murder aroused great indignation among the Russian[2] population of Kiev. The investigation into the case was initially conducted by Medvedev, a district judicial investigator. The corpse was examined and the autopsy performed by Karpinsky, a police doctor. After the extremely mysterious nature of the crime became apparent, the case was entrusted to Special Judicial Investigator V.I. Fenenko. At his request, a new and very thorough autopsy of Yushchinsky's corpse was performed by N.A. Obolonsky, Professor of Forensic Medicine, assisted by Prosector N.N. Tufanov.

The police in charge of the investigation initially suspected that Yushchinsky had been murdered by his mother (married name, Prikhodko), but her innocence was then fully established.

So who killed Andrei Yushchinsky? The investigation established that he had not simply been killed: he had been tortured to death. 45 stab wounds[3] were found on the body, in a number of different locations. These stab wounds, as firmly established by the forensic medical examination, were inflicted with three tools: a knife 1.5 cm in width, a 4-sided nail (which had been driven into the skull as well), and a thin piercing tool similar to an awl. These facts clearly show the participation of several persons in the torture-murder.

The victim's body had been entirely drained of blood (as a result of which, the corpse decomposed very little over the two-week period prior to its discovery[4]). The body was drained of blood while the victim

---

[1] *Novoye Vremya*, April 14, 1911, No. 12602. – *I.I. Lyutostansky*.
[2] That is, non-Jewish. – *Translator's Note*.
[3] 47 is the correct number. – *Translator's Note*.
[4] From the murder to the second autopsy. – *Translator's Note*.

was still alive, because all [47] of the stab wounds were inflicted pre-mortem. While the boy was tortured and exsanguinated, he, as firmly established by Professor N.A. Obolonsky, was held in a standing position (because the blood flowed downwards, lengthwise along the body). The boy was naked. His shirt was the only item of clothing not removed [by the killers]; rather, it was pulled up and unbuttoned. The boy's hands were tightly tied together by the wrists, behind his back, with a thin rope, and his mouth was shut (so tightly that signs of strangulation appeared; also, bite marks were found on the inner parts of the lips). The neck veins were cut open with a knife, and blood was drawn from them.

As already mentioned, all 47 of the stab wounds were inflicted while the victim was still alive; seven stab wounds were present on the left side of the chest, in the region of the heart; the boy was killed with these latter deep wounds, or pricks, after the blood had been drained from the body. The corpse was dressed after death: not a drop of blood was found on any of his clothing (it is precisely this fact which proves that the boy was dressed *after* death); only the shirt was blood-stained, because it had not been removed [during commission of the crime].

The corpse was not buried; rather, it was laid out on the ground in a small cave. The victim was already dead when brought to the cave, but rigor mortis had not yet set in, as firmly established by Professor Obolonsky and Prosector Tufanov – that is, the boy was murdered at night and moved to the cave before dawn.[1]

---

[1] This is not quite true. The investigation established that the boy was murdered in the daytime, and that rigor mortis had already set in when his corpse was brought to the cave. An accurate and comprehensive account of this case can be found in *The Murder of Andrei Yushchinsky* by G.G. Zamyslovsky. – *Translator's Note*.

The Ritual Murder in Trent

This Nuremberg engraving dates back to the 15th century and depicts the making of incisions on the body of Saint Simon of Trent, in a room adjacent to the synagogue, on March 24, 1475, on Thursday of Holy Week.

It is noteworthy that 400 years ago, people already knew how to make incisions in a "tender and loving" manner, so that the child would remain alive until all his blood was drawn. Yet, our modern professors, on the basis of the incisions made [to Vintsenta Grudzinskaya] with a "tender and loving hand", rejected the ritual murder accusation brought against Blondes.

Ippolit Iosifovich Lyutostansky

- the-savoisien.com
- pdfarchive.info
- vivaeuropa.info
- freepdf.info
- aryanalibris.com
- aldebaranvideo.tv
- histoireebook.com
- balderexlibris.com

www.ingramcontent.com/pod-product-compliance
Lightning Source LLC
LaVergne TN
LVHW041544060526
838200LV00037B/1131